P9-CNE-597

MY HUSBAND KEEPS TELLING ME
TO GO TO HELL

OTHER BOOKS BY ELLA BENTLEY ARTHUR

SONNY BOY'S DAY AT THE ZOO
SONGS OF A CREOLE CITY
DEAR DOROTHY DIX, with Harnett T. Kane

OTHER BOOKS BY HARNETT T. KANE

LOUISIANA HAYRIDE, *The American Rehearsal for Dictatorship*
BAYOUS OF LOUISIANA
DEEP DELTA COUNTRY *(In the American Folkways Series)*
PLANTATION PARADE, *The Grand Manner in Louisiana*
NEW ORLEANS WOMAN, *Biographical Novel of Myra Clark Gaines*
NATCHEZ ON THE MISSISSIPPI
BRIDE OF FORTUNE, *Novel Based on the Life of Mrs. Jefferson Davis*
QUEEN NEW ORLEANS, *City by the River*
PATHWAY TO THE STARS, *Novel Based on the Life of John McDonogh*
THE SCANDALOUS MRS. BLACKFORD, *Novel Based on the Life of
    Mrs. Harriet Blackford*
GENTLEMEN, SWORDS AND PISTOLS
DEAR DOROTHY DIX, *The Story of a Compassionate Woman*
    (In Collaboration with Ella Bentley Arthur)
THE LADY OF ARLINGTON, *Novel Based on the Life of
    Mrs. Robert E. Lee*

My husband keeps

Illustrations by R. TAYLOR

Hanover House

telling me to go to Hell

By ELLA BENTLEY ARTHUR

Introduction by HARNETT T. KANE

GARDEN CITY, NEW YORK

Copyright 1954 by Ella Bentley Arthur and Harnett T. Kane

Illustrations copyright 1954 by Richard Taylor

Library of Congress Catalog Card Number: 54-5762

Printed in the United States of America
First Edition

HOW THIS BOOK CAME ABOUT

by Harnett T. Kane

Ever since all of America (or the part of it with a sensitive funny bone) greeted the publication of the famous "Boners" books in the early thirties, the country has been waiting for another book that would have something of the same appeal, much of the same wise-naive implications.

Here, it seems to me, is precisely that book, with a bit more—its own special flavoring, a unique coloration in its own right.

For more than a half century the late Dorothy Dix, who was called everything from America's Mother Confessor to "a wise old mountain goat," received questions that covered every conceivable difficulty that man or woman (woman, especially) ever met.

Her mail totaled thousands of items a day, on perfumed sheets, engraved paper, penny post cards, legal brief sheets, the back of grocery-store fly sheets. It came from Girl Scouts and Geisha girls (many Orientals wrote her), maidens with fallen hopes, matrons with fallen chests and/or arches; it came also from plain men, with problems no less vivid than those of the ladies.

During nearly twenty-five years a younger woman, Miss Dix's friend and associate, worked near her, opening the letters, culling and classifying them, talking them over with her. That friend, Ella Bentley Arthur of New Orleans, made a kind of hobby out of her analysis of these letters from the columnist's 60,000,000 readers.

From time to time—once or twice a day, once a month, in dry spells—Mrs. Arthur's eyes brightened with a gleam of discovery. Here was a strange and mirth-stirring query, or a marvel of English construction, or a subject presented in a way that no humorist, perspiring for hours, could have concocted.

"Boners," Miss Dix and Mrs. Arthur sometimes called them; yet they were not quite that. "Malapropisms," perhaps; but that name does not cover them precisely. They were not intended to be funny in any fashion; many arose as cries from the heart, appeals touching or disturbing in their simplicity. They had sharpness, originality, often a rare pungency.

Here follow some of the best of these passages from a phenomenal correspondence, a small percentage taken from a collection of uncounted thousands. They have been chosen to demonstrate nothing, to prove nothing of great significance. They are offered as a cross section of the American mind or mood, or as examples of American ability

8

to handle the English language in a way that the Lords never intended.

They do show one thing, perhaps, often shown before—the thin line of division between tragedy and comedy, between shattering disaster and the plain prattfall.

Some grow out of simple misunderstanding, or misconception, of the dictionary definition of words; others are so apt that they make the reader decide the dictionary is the one which is wrong. Still others have a direct conviction that transcends mundane definition of certain terms, or conventional conceptions of such terms.

"We just got married on the spree of the moment," writes a girl. Who could say it better? A youth asks what to do for his pimples, because he has "what is known today as an inferiority complexion." Who could improve on that?

There is a world of secondary meaning in many of these notes. "My husband is colder than an electric refrigerator; how can I defrost him?" asks a wife. In the same way a dissatisfied miss complains that her sweetheart has "been dormant for three months."

And few, premeditating for days, could have achieved the chaste beauty of: "My husband keeps telling me to go to Hell. Have I a legal right to take the children?"

On many occasions, in letters and verbally, Dorothy Dix approved Ella Arthur's intention of gathering these selections in book form. Frequently Miss Dix read them to audiences; again Mrs. Arthur did. Each time the original material was chosen by Mrs. Arthur, and often Miss Dix expressed her admiration for her friend's skill, which in time became almost instinctive, in picking out the stray phrase, the rambling sentence with its gem of phrasing.

These quotations have been the subject of considerable curiosity, of inquiries and requests for "full copies" after people heard them at occasional meetings. Once or twice Mrs. Arthur discovered shorthand stenographers assigned at gatherings to take them down surreptitiously. Only recently, after this writer and Mrs. Arthur discussed their book, *Dear Dorothy Dix,* at a meeting in a large Southern city, one breathless individual stepped up to demand a "complete set" of them.

"My husband is a doctor," the lady smiled. "You know how doctors are. He'd like to tell them all to his patients, or at the next convention."

The lady did not get them. But, in case she remains interested, here are some of them, with others that Doc may want to tell.

MY HUSBAND KEEPS TELLING ME
TO GO TO HELL

Should a girl sit on her boy friend's lap in his coupe if there isn't room for her on his seat?

Our club is giving a dance at the hotel. I have a gray sleeveless dress and a black one with long sleeves. Which shall I wear, if any?

There is a great void in my life to be filled, so I have fallen in love with a dentist.

I am in love with a married man. About a year ago we had a misunderstanding and as a result his wife has a three-months-old baby.

I'm in love with a married man and we try to be as thoughtful as possible of his wife and arrange our meetings on lodge nights.

He was electrocuted once and it nearly killed him.

Should we have our marriage consummated
by a photographer?

I am awkward and ill at ease with my girl friend and have great trouble in finding some place to put my hands. Please tell me where to keep them.

Do you consider it a crime for married people to commit adultery with those of the opposing sex?

I am a girl 25 years old and instead of marrying I am planning to go to college, and get a B. A. degree; but would a B. A. degree give you the same satisfaction a husband would?

Miss Dix, is my boy friend a good Catholic or is he trying to get rid of me? He has given me up for Lent.

What I feel for her is not really love. I think
it is what they call inflation.

The doctors have diagnosed my case a nervous prostitution.

He told me to give in or walk home and as it was raining hard and I didn't have a raincoat, what was there for me to do?

My wife having died a month ago I sent a card of thanks to all our relatives and friends.

I am a young girl who has disgraced herself by having a baby, and he certainly is cute!

18

I don't want to date him, but he is continually coming over and rapeing at my door.

I read the other day that every 7th child born into the world was Chinese. Oh, please help me, Miss Dix; I am about to have my 7th child!

We fight like cat and dog and he curses me something awful. His birthday is September 15th and mine is May 12th. Are we congenial?

Will you please tell an anxious groom the first words to say to his bride upon coming out of the church with her, and how to entertain her later.

I have never gone wrong, Miss Dix, as fortunately I know none of the facts of life. Will you please tell me where I can get the information?

My baby's navel has a downcast appear-
ance. How can I naturalize it?

My husband has a disease called gondolier.

My husband keeps telling me to go to Hell.
Have I a legal right to take the children?

She drives her own car, wears a fur coat and in fact lives like any other stenographer. ˙

As soon as he comes into the house he says "What the hell are you doing here? Who in the hell wants you? Get the hell out of here." He also uses profane language.

Shall I tell my husband the baby I am expecting is not his? Please answer before Labor Day.

Everybody respects her—an ideal girl, the kind fellows put on a pillow.

Please help me. I am a Canadian girl in love
with the mounted police.

I am 16 years old and a boy took advantage of my knowing nothing of the facts of life by telling me we were going blackberrying in the woods.

Please tell me what to do for pimples. I have what is known today as an inferiority complexion.

I am not exactly engaged but have had an affair-de-car.

I have just found out that the man I am engaged to is already married. Wouldn't I be justified in breaking our engagement?

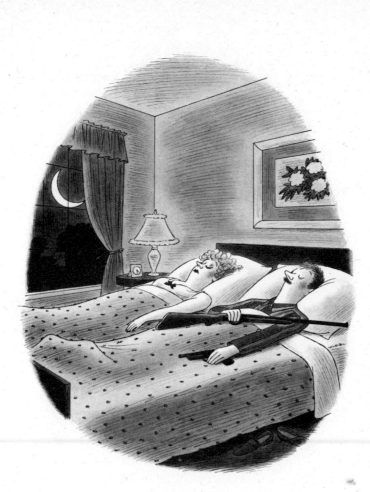

I am a widow who cannot be comfortable
unless sleeping with a man in the house for
protection.

I know he loves me because he kissed me on the back seat.

He says he wants to marry me in the worst way and you know, Miss Dix, that means without a wedding ring.

Everybody warned me he would seduce me but I wouldn't believe them, so I found out the hard way.

My son-in-law is an expected father, and my daughter is an approaching mother.

My husband has a bad case of indolent fever.

I am a diabetic, and my boy friend is
against my being a diabetic.

I am a widow whose only son has just
taken his screen test for the Army.

I married a man who is a hopeless cripple
and walks on crutches, but in no time he
began stepping out on me.

I don't mind my boy friend hitting me, which he does whenever it suits him. But when he knocks me down in the street, I think that is making our love too public.

I heard her husband knocked her down in their garden. So you see her life is not all a bed of roses.

We went out for a walk and to have a bite. Don't misunderstand me, Miss Dix, I mean something to eat.

I am in love with a man who is not of my religion or nationality. He is divorced, a hard drinker and 35 years my senior. Do you think I should marry him and if so, what color dress should I wear?

My boy friend is always running after other girls—in other words, he has a bad case of female trouble.

Owing to circumstances over which I had no control, I became the mother of three children born out of wedlock.

All symptoms during our courtship pointed to a happy mirage.

What position do a bride and bridegroom take when they get to the altar and what position when they return home?

I am brokenhearted because my daughter wants to marry a boy who is not of our religion, who hasn't a job or a penny to his name. How can I stop her from marrying him, and on which side does the bride's mother sit?

34

I am going to be married and am putting
aside everything I can for my goose egg.

He told me he was crazy about me and that he would never be able to live without me; in fact, he even talked of marriage.

We had a terrible fight, and if we ever make it up, it will be nothing short of a coincidence.

Mine is an ideal marriage. We were wed three months ago and now I have a fine baby boy.

The boy I am crazy about never comes to see me, never asks for a date, never notices me at all. Tell me, Miss Dix, does he love me deep down in his heart?

Women are destined to be the futuristic leaders of this country.

I think marriage is the termination of life.

I am not married because I have always thought it is better to live a singular life than a plural one.

I am going to have a baby by a boy I met just a few weeks ago. I can't marry him, as he is practically a stranger and it would be taking too great a risk.

Please advise about my wedding and just exactly what the cortege should consist of.

I stutter very badly. Should I tell my fiance?

His marriage lasted ten months and then a divorce succeeded.

Though I have beautiful hips and bust I am not a success with boys as I also have high ideals.

I want to have my nose remodeled by a plastic seargeant. Send me the address of one so that I can have it done by return mail.

Is marriage the real route to concubinal—or is the word conjugal—bliss?

The older generation is always running us down for the necking parties we throw; but when you're tired of movies, dances and bright lights, what else is there to do?

He wanted to get married as he thought that was one way for us to get better acquainted.

I have two children, a dog, cat, and a seven-room house to take care of, not counting a husband.

Of course, I gave in to him as I am very weak when I want to be.

Of course my wife and I have spats like all happily married couples, and I once broke her ribs. But we have never had any disagreement of a serious nature.

You speak of girls having a technique with boys. Just where do you buy this technique and how do you use it?

My mother saved us from being raised in the traditional Southern way of growing up with only average intelligence.

I am 16 years old and a wife in fact only.

I had a date with my boy friend and on the way home he said let's get married or something. But I read your column, Miss Dix, and I said, let's get married or nothing.

She has been going with nobody since she's been going with me.

I blame my mother for my misfortune. If
she had instilled in me the right principles
of birth control, I would not now be the
mother of an unwed baby.

Just what are the duties of a bridegroom
after the ceremony has been performed?

I am what others consider an intelligent young bachelor as I have never married.

You don't know how prejudiced mothers can be, Miss Dix. My mother didn't like him simply and solely because he mistreated me.

I would like you to help me as you have helped others in trouble. The trouble is I'm married.

I know you think I am making a monument out of a molehill.

I am a young girl greatly desiring the company of the object sex.

I have six children by my present husband,
who is of a cold and frigid nature.

At a fashionable wedding would you suggest two matrons and two patrons of honor, and is there any distinction regarding the length of their married life?

God saw fit to take my husband from me and left me crushed and heartbroken. Please send me the names of some eligible bachelors.

He asked me to marry him Saturday night and I was all ready to do so but he didn't come so my evening was spoiled.

I am a good and faithful husband and never give in to a girl unless I can't help myself.

My wife has a goitre but her expensive way
of living and trying to be an Episcopalian
has kept us from having it removed.

Our neighbors say our chickens ruined their garden. Well, it's a 50-50 proposition, Miss Dix. Their son ruined our daughter.

All he did was brain work, and you know
yourself, Miss Dix, that isn't hard.

He wanted to kiss me, hug me, etc., and I refused. I guess you think that's funny for a modern girl, but it was really the etc. that I objected to.

Can you have freckles and sex appeal at the same time?

My big sister is now having an affair with an old man of 35 or 40.

I am not very good looking at the side view but am handsome in front.

I read your articles until I had a nervous breakdown.

I have been an adolescent for the past six or seven years. When will I grow up to be an adultress?

I am supposed to get food, clothing and gasoline from 12 chickens and a cow.

I read your articles on how to be a perfect lady and as a result am home every night.

I have led about as impeccable a life as could be expected of a Navy man.

In a tete-a-tete with my wife she called me a damn fool.

I love my sweetheart but I am a virtuous girl and will never do the wrong thing till the right time comes.

I have a friend who is stone deaf and my heart bleeds for her as she cannot hear any of the disagreeable things her family are constantly saying about her.

I would like a home, husband, and babies, but what are you going to do when you live in a town where all the boys are too young to supply these deficiencies?

He struck me such a terrible blow in the
stomach it raised a whelp.

The man who ruined me has dark eyes, dark hair and a Chevrolet coupe.

Will you please tell me all the facts of life and send me the addresses of some soldiers and sailors?

My girl friend likes to drink some, dance and pet —in fact I really think I have found my ideal girl.

My husband is a highly respected citizen of his community, having been defeated for county chairman three successive times.

I am 23 and he is 58, and I want to be a comfort to him in his reclining years.

When I returned home I found my girl in a house of prostitution, and, of course, Miss Dix, in your profession you know what that means.

I would like to have your definition of a perfect lady—I must have it before this weekend.

I had the most tactful of stepmothers. She died ten years ago.

I am interested in being a nice girl and well thought of, but not, of course, if it is going to interfere with my popularity.

My husband is a middle-age philanderer; in other words, one of those second-hand, re-conditioned sheiks.

For the enclosed five cents please send me
self-confidence and sex appeal.

Her ex-husband has a milk and egg busi-
ness, and is now demanding the custard of
the child.

She took a trip with a man who is married and has a five year old daughter by auto.

Unfortunately I am one of those husbands who has no women friends to be crooked with.

Are a radio, a car and a television set everything in life—or can a determined couple get along on less?

He has been a perfect gentleman toward me, which I did not expect from a married man.

I have been a decent girl, as far as I remember.

He wants to date me for a night club but
how can I accept when I have no night
dress?

What's the use trying to keep up appearances when we haven't any?

I am a 50-year-old man in love with a woman who already has a husband. Please suggest the quickest and most humane way of getting rid of same.

All her relatives are dead, so now she feels she can settle down to happiness.

Shall I go out and look for a job, or stay at home until I find the lucky man?

We are three girls and have an outrageous question to ask you.

I think my husband has been trifling on me. I came home from a week-end visit and found a pair of stockings, powder, and rouge pot that weren't mine in the bedroom. Are my suspicions unfounded?

I have a baby who looks like our milkman, and so my husband beats me up every night. How can I prove to him that all I get from the milkman is milk?

I have a sweetheart but he has been dormant for three months.

My father wants me to stay home till I am twenty-
one. What will good times mean to me then when
my youth is wasted and gone?

My wife's death left me spellbound.

I would like very much to know what time you
think a girl almost 14 and a freshman in high
school should go to bed.

How can I prove to my two model daughters that
virtue is its own reward when what they both want
is to be married?

My husband works for a baking powder
company, and naturally rises early.

What I asked for was a divorce and my maiden name back but the court gave me all the children. There is no justice for mothers any more.

My father's confinement was responsible for my birth. He was confined in an insane asylum.

Miss Dix, does a girl do wrong to kiss a boy the first time she mates him?

The reason why the doctor can tell so soon that I am pregnant is because I have been under him for three months.

Is there any harm in a girl sitting in a car
with a boy if you know how to behave from
11 to 2 in the morning?

My husband beats me, bloodies my nose, bruises my arms, slaps me hard enough to leave prints on my face, kicks my legs and leaves me alone at nights. I know this doesn't sound like much, Miss Dix, but you can't imagine how I dislike it.

I am a married woman and have no children as far as I know. You see I have no idea what my husband did before I married him.

I am so much in love I can't eat, sleep, or constipate on anything.

We just got married on the spree of the moment.

I am crazy about a boy who is one hundred per cent impossible.

I know she has a bad character, but my husband says she is the purest woman that ever walked the streets.